© Copyrights

This book is dedicated to:

"To my beloved daughter and supportive partner,

You both have been the guiding stars in my world, helping to light every step in this journey. Your belief in me, your encouragement, and your patience have been my strength.

This book is a testament to the unwavering amount of support and love you have generously showered upon me. Your presence in my life has been the inspiration behind every word written. With love and gratitude, I dedicate these pages to you for being my pillars of strength.

With all my love and appreciation.

Acknowledgment

We are profoundly grateful to our dearest family and friends, whose support and understanding have been the cornerstone of the book's creation.

To our family, your patience, encouragement, and constant belief in our endeavors have been an endless source of strength.

Your encouragement and unwavering belief in our capabilities have been invaluable to our friends.

We want to express our heartfelt gratitude to each one of you. Your belief in our vision has been instrumental in bringing this book to fruition. Your constant presence and faith in us have made this possible.

Thank you for shining bright and helping us towards the light.

With most profound appreciation and love.

About the Author

The authors are a mother-daughter duo who love sharing positive messages with everyone reading their stories.

 Addisen is a bright young girl who believes everyone is unique and has something to share.

 Terresa believes in inspiring everyone to reach their full potential and never abandon their dreams.

This book is Gumball's very first adventure. He will have to believe In himself and gain his magical wings.

Gumball was a small dragon who was growing up so fast.

Gumball was worried about a test that was coming up in ten days.

When a dragon turns six, they are given a flying test. They must fly to a magical flower named Penelope to gain their magical wings.

All the young dragons had to fly to the next city where Penelope was and fly back.

Once they reached Penelope, she would smile at all the young dragons who made it to her and give them their magical wings.

His best friend's name is Dandelion, and she will also take the test in ten days. She was a good flier already.

With only eight days left until the test, Dandelion asked Gumball if he wanted to fly that day. Gumball declined, saying he might be up for it tomorrow. Disappointed, Dandelion said, "Okay," and flew away.

Dandelion often invited Gumball to fly with her occasionally, but he was nervous because he had never flown that far. He didn't think he could do it, and with only eight days until the big test, he was very nervous.

Dandelion knew Gumball needed to believe in himself, and he would pass. Dandelion went to Gumball again the next day and asked, "Would you like to fly today? Again, Gumball said, "No, thank you, I don't think I can today."

Whenever Dandelion asked Gumball to fly with her for the next four days, he would reply, "No, thank you, not today."

But four days before the flying test, Gumball closed his eyes, took a deep breath, and decided to try flying alone.

He began to believe in himself. On his first attempt, he flew past two houses and returned to his home.

He was very proud of himself and decided to try to go even further tomorrow.

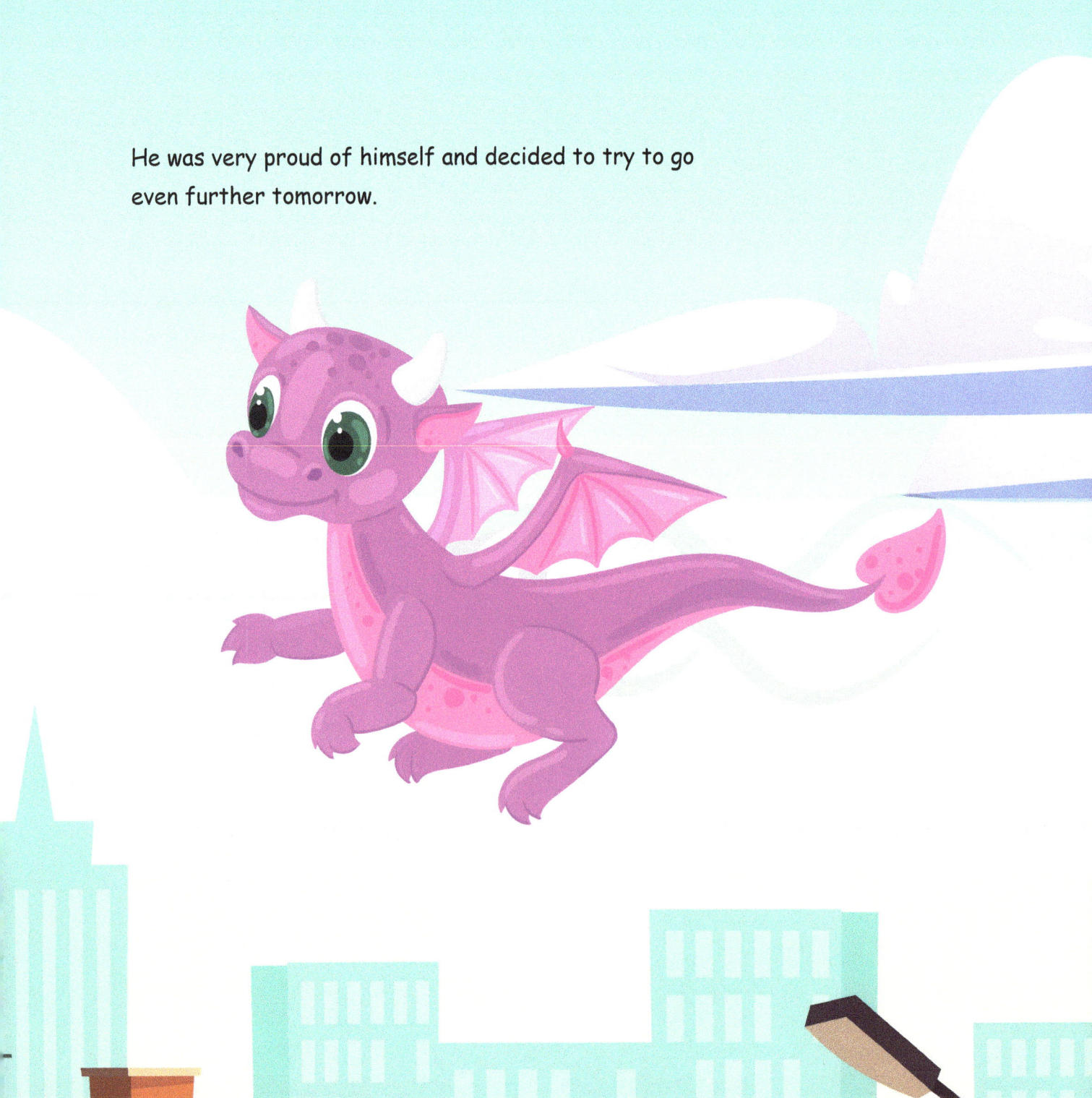

Three days before the test, Gumball flew farther than he did the day before. He was starting to feel that he would be able to earn his magical wings. He was also feeling more confident in himself.

Finally, the big day was here. Gumball saw that Dandelion was already lined up with the other child dragons, and he was so excited to see her.

Dandelion asked Gumball, "How do you feel today?" Gumball replied, "I am very nervous but can do it." Dandelion said, "We are going to have an amazing day."

As soon as the race started, Gumball became discouraged. He was beginning to fall behind all the other dragons, afraid he would not reach Penelope (the magical flower).

As soon as he was about to give up and turn around, he saw Dandelion in front of him.

She smiled back at him and said, "We are almost to Penelope!".

Gumball could not believe it; he was so excited when he saw Penelope right before him.

As he got closer to Penelope, she smiled and winked at Gumball. The next thing Gumball knew, his wings started to glow, and he flew faster than ever.

Dandelion and Gumball were so happy that they had earned their magical wings. All Gumball had to do was believe in himself.

The rest of the day was full of celebration and excitement.
Gumball will never forget the day he believed in himself and earned his magical wings.

Believe in yourself
By Terresa
Never doubt how strong you are
Even when things seem tough
Remember to shine bright like a star
Keep pushing forward when things seem rough
Try hard in everything you do
Don't ever give up, believe in you.

The End

www.ingramcontent.com/pod-product-compliance
Lightning Source LLC
Chambersburg PA
CBHW051322110526
44590CB00031B/4445